THE TWELVE STAGES OF HUMILITY

Adapted from John McQuiston's
Always We Begin Again

The
Meditation
ॐ Series

The Rule of Saint Benedict is a set of directions for monastic life written by Benedict of Nursia in the sixth century in Italy. The Rule has been largely lost in our time. However, John McQuiston II, a busy Memphis attorney and lay leader in the Episcopal church, was searching for a truly balanced life. He found the blueprint for it in this ancient text. McQuiston interpreted and restated Benedict's system of spiritual living, enabling today's reader to understand and make use of its remarkable insights.

The "Twelve Stages of Humility" is but one chapter in the text. Copies of the entire reinterpretation of the rule — *Always We Begin Again* — can be purchased from Morehouse Publishing, 4775 Linglestown Road, Harrisburg, PA 17112.

TO BE EXALTED
IS TO BE IN DANGER

HUMILITY

Cultivate humility.
To be exalted is to be in danger.

Pride is considered a sin because it
warps our existence.
It established our lives on a false foundation.

No one can win all the time.
Therefore, a life based on triumphing over
others will always be unfulfilled.

The way to closeness with the sublime
is not to add.
It is to take away each day
until we have been freed,
even from the desire for perfection.

THE
TWELVE
STAGES
OF
HUMILITY

These are the stages to freedom from
self-centeredness,
to humility,
the centerpiece of the true life.

EVERY MOMENT
WE LIVE IN IS IRREPLACEABLE

1

The first stage of humility
is to keep the sacred nature of consciousness
and the world in which it exists
always alive within us.

Everything we think,
everything we do,
everything we feel,
is cast in time forever.
Every moment that we live is irreplaceable,
therefore each moment is hallowed.

We must be on guard
against despair, against fear,
against bitterness, against self-seeking,
and have the tenacity and courage
to think optimistically and act kindly,
and to put the needs of others
always before our own.

OUR DESIRES
ARE THE PATH TO DISASTER

2

The second stage of humility
is to distrust our own will.
Our wants are insatiable
and our will is the product of those wants.
Our pleasure,
our needs,
our wishes —
all are mere self-interest,
and the demands of self-interest are never ending.

Our desires are the path to disaster.
At every turn there is something more to acquire,
something to distract our attention,
something to divert the unchangeable.

Day and night we must return to humility,
and use it as a compass to guide us on
the true course.

Therefore the second stage of humility
is not to love our own will,
nor to find pleasure in the satisfaction of
our own desires,
but to carry our the unfathomable purpose
of our being, to fulfill the design that can only
be discovered by overcoming our own cravings —
for the function of existence,
and of our lives,
is not ourselves.

OUR WILL
WILL NOT BE DONE

3

The third stage of humility
is to accept our limitations,
even to death.

To accept that there are events
outside our control
and that have ultimate power over us,
and that our will
will not be done.

BE THANKFUL
EVEN FOR INJURIES

4

The fourth stage of humility
is to be patient
and to maintain a quiet mind,
even in the face of inequity, injury,
and contradiction,
preserving the awareness
that we are ever shaped by
experience
and refined by fire,
and accordingly
to be thankful even for injuries.

NOT TO
CONCEAL OUR FAULTS

5

The fifth stage of humility
is not to conceal our faults,
but to be ruthlessly honest
with ourselves,
for to lie to ourselves or to others
is to falsify our relationship with true life.

NOTHING THAT OCCURS TO US
IS INTRINSICALLY GOOD OR BAD

6

The sixth stage of humility
is to be content
with the work we are given to do
and with the circumstances of our lives
however unfair or demeaning,
always bearing in mind
that it is our outlook
that confers value on our experience,
and that nothing that occurs to us
is intrinsically good or bad.

TO BELIEVE THAT WE ARE
OF NO CONSEQUENCE

7

The seventh stage of humility
is not only to declare ourselves to be humble,
but to believe in our hearts that we are
of no consequence.

For alone we are of no moment —
in the vast reaches and endless
memory of the universe
our most profound idea is the merest fantasy;
our greatest triumphs
and our meanest actions
are as lasting as a footprint in the sand.

ALWAYS MISTRUSTING
OUR OWN IDEAS AND WILLS

8

The eighth stage of humility
is that we take no action except that which is
in accordance with the path established for
us, by word and by example, by those whom
we know to be true guides, both past and
present, always mistrusting our own ideas
and wills.

REFRAIN
FROM JUDGMENT

9

The ninth stage of humility
is that we refrain from judgment.

It is not for us to live the lives of others,
or to understand the infinite forces at work
at every instant in another's life.

We must restrain not only in our criticism
but also our advice,
offering it only when requested,
and then only with sincere misgiving.

TO HAVE
SINCERE EMPATHY

10

The tenth stage of humility
is to have sincere empathy.

We can never believe ourselves superior
to another,
nor take pleasure in each other's
shortcomings and misfortunes.

SPEAK GENTLY
AND BRIEFLY

11

The eleventh stage of humility
is to speak gently and briefly.

Participation in community requires
that we speak and also that we listen.

In speech we must be candid,
in listening we must be accessible.

MAINTAIN A
HUMBLE DEMEANOR

12

The twelfth stage of humility
is to maintain not only humble thoughts,
but also a humble demeanor,
whether at work, on the road, at
the market,
in speaking
or at rest.

We should continuously reenforce,
through appearance and demeanor, the
mien of humility.

By daily pursuing these intentions,
we will begin to observe these precepts
through habit rather than by discipline,
and in consequence,
after long practice,
we will sometimes accomplish these goals
as our natural manner.

Made in the USA
Columbia, SC
15 December 2018